MW00804099

What Matters Publishing House

letters from
GOD

Journal

Daily conversations with God

Scripture quotations marked AMP are from The Amplified Bible, Old Testament
copyright © 1965, 1987 by the Zondervan Corporation. The Amplified Bible, New
Testament copyright © 1954, 1958, 1987 by The Lockman Foundation. Used by
permission. All rights reserved.

Unless otherwise indicated, all scripture quotations are from The Holy Bible, English
Standard Version® (ESV®). Copyright ©2001 by Crossway Bibles, a division of
Good News Publishers. Used by
permission. All rights reserved.

Scripture quotations marked KJV are from the Holy Bible, King James Version (Au-
thorized Version). First published in 1611. Quoted from the KJV Classic Reference
Bible, Copyright © 1983 by The Zondervan Corporation.

Scripture quotations marked MSG are taken from The Message. Copyright © 1993,
1994, 1995, 1996, 2000, 2001, 2002, 2003 by Eugene H. Peterson. Used by permission of NavPress Publishing Group. Website.

Scripture quotations marked NASB are taken from the New American Standard
Bible®, Copyright © 1960, 1962, 1963, 1968, 1971, 1972, 1973, 1975, 1977, 1995
by The Lockman Foundation. Used by permission.

Scripture quotations marked NIV are taken from the Holy Bible, New International
Version®. NIV®. Copyright © 1973, 1978, 1984 by International Bible Society.
Used by permission of Zondervan. All rights reserved.

Scripture quotations marked "NKJV™" are taken from the New King James Ver-
sion®. Copyright © 1982 by Thomas Nelson, Inc. Used by permission. All rights
reserved.

Scripture quotations marked RSV are taken from the Revised Standard Version of the
Bible, copyright © 1946, 1952, 1971 by the Division of Christian Education of the
National Council of the Churches of Christ in the USA. Used by permission.

Scripture quotations marked TLB are taken from The Living Bible copyright ©
1971. Used by
permission of Tyndale House Publishers, Inc., Carol Stream, Illinois 60188. All
rights reserved.

Published by
What Matters Ministries and Missions Publishing
ISBN-10   098930602X
ISBN-13   978-0-9893060-2-7

Design and Layout: What Matters Ministries and Missions

Printed in the United States of America

A Note From The Author

The Quest

The life of journaling releases the elements of destiny, harness-es the wild thoughts, and brings the truth into focus. It gives your conscience a megaphone. There are many types of journaling, a few of which are outlined below. As you begin to use your pen to expose your heart, your motives, your feelings, your relationships, your struggles, the good, the bad, and the ugly, you will begin to develop each type.

Intimacy journaling melds you into God and disconnects you from falsehood, insincerity, and pretending. It releases you to begin to experience the secret parts of God and the secret parts of your-self—ones that are veiled, hidden, or afraid to come into the light. *Relationship journaling* exposes the fears you have of entering into relationships with other people, even with God. As you write, you heal and repair the past and broken relationships of your life by allowing the Holy Spirit to literally speak His healing words through your pen.

Journaling is a journey through the path of restoration, release, and discovery. It affirms to you what God has already revealed, healed, and sealed in your heart. It is the discovery of your Author flowing out of your pen. Each type of journaling heals a piece of you. *For-giveness journaling,* for example, allows you to say things on paper that your mouth cannot actually utter. It enables you to forgive people whom you vowed long ago to never forgive, releasing you from the self-imposed jail sentence that you have placed on yourself.

Clarity is the eye of journaling, bringing everything into focus. It drives away the confusion fog that loves to follow people around. In order to self-heal, create and perfect the art of opening your veins and letting the truth speak. Allow the Holy Spirit to do His work in your heart as you renounce the fear of truth and instead journey into reality and freedom. When you pick up your pen and let the false counselor die, you open your soul to the words and winds of power; you spread your wings and soar into God's arms. *Love journaling* is a voyage into the very heart of that which is wounded. It ventures to the place where the love of God can fill the hollow caverns of your soul. There, God's love paints the true destiny that He has created for you. Journaling is the paintbrush and, with each stroke, transforms you to be love-ruled and destiny-driven.

As you write, you redefine yourself; you separate the precious from the vile, and you expose the wolves in sheep's clothing. On the days when you vent and repent, you reposition yourself for favor, blessing, and promotion. Journaling is God's broom as it forces destruction into the open and annihilates it. Never settle for half-truth living. When you practice genuineness in your written words, you tear the mask off of your false destinies. You remove the possibility of deceiving yourself. Stand back and listen to the truth, and let its medicine flow out of your heart. Refreshment, encouragement, and hope will never leave your life when you shut the door on denial and open the door to trust. As you let your heart speak, you must let truth be the umpire. The heart is a masterless slave and must be trained to love truth. Capturing your thoughts on paper does just that. It will never fail you whether you are faith journaling, dream journaling, or weeding your soul, for there is no negative aspect to God-ruled journaling.

On the following pages, there are examples for those of you who have never discovered the joy of writing out the beautiful and ugly truth on paper or on your computer screen. Begin writing today, and give God permission to redefine you.

EXAMPLE

October 29

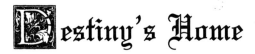

Destiny's Home

Isaiah 42:9
*Behold, the former things are come to pass, and new
things do I declare: before they spring forth I tell you of them.*
KJV

How did I become a professional gravedigger? You say the past is in the grave where it belongs, but I constantly go back and bury myself up to my knees, wallowing in my former sin, acting as if it is still alive and well. Why can't I forgive myself entirely? Why am I so attached to shame? I still feel stained. I long for my memory to be cleansed. I long to be fully free from the chains of the past. I long to have the feelings of guilt subside. It's as if I don't feel worthy of complete wholeness. I consider it my duty to work my way into cleanliness, to examine the grave, to dig up the worms and try to eliminate them myself. I am unable. Help me see the future with clarity and deny the past a place in my life from this point forward. Take me out of yesterday's reach. Heal me entirely so I can be a voice to other gravediggers. You alone are able. I believe.

EXAMPLE

January 24

I Am Passing By

Matthew 9:22
*Daughter, be of good comfort; thy faith hath made thee whole.
And the woman was made whole from that hour.*
KJV

God, allow me to be tied to you and you alone. May I not miss you when you are so near. May I not be blind to your presence or deaf to your voice. When the waves come and roar and crash may you be my focus and my call. Thank you for watching for me, for noticing my gentle graze of your hem as I extend all I am to meet all that you are. Thank you for having already crossed every bridge and calmed every storm that there would be nothing between myself and you.

EXAMPLE

July 20

The Miry Clay

Psalm 40:2
He brought me up also out of an horrible pit, out of the miry clay, and set my feet upon a rock, and established my goings. KJV

God draws us upward, never pushes us down.
Miry: (Strong's) mire (Webster's) wet spongy earth; troublesome or intractable situation
Clay: (Strong's) mud (Webster's) an earthy material that is plastic when moist but hard when fired

This reminds me of where I was when I accepted Jesus. Searching, not confident in where I was or my future. Speaks to me about people who are not "set" in their ways, still searching. God knows if we've been "fired" and set or are still able to be released from what is trying to mold us.
Beautiful that he delivers us from being normal or common, molded, and teaches us to fly, walk, and run. Then He gives us eyes for others that are slowly drifting away from "the reach of Love's hands." "Floating on their weak rafts" ...so true.
Note: study out "Established my goings"

EXAMPLE

ᴅaptured by Heaven's Smile

Numbers 6:24-26
The Lord bless you and keep you; the Lord make His face shine upon you, and be gracious to you; the Lord lift up His countenance upon you, and give you peace.
NKJV

Dear Lord! You are too good to me! I love You, I love You, I love You! I want what You speak over me, but I feel captured by so many things! I am trying to fight against this addiction, but I feel myself hungering more for it. I know You want me to stop. I know You have better things for me. I love You for it, but God, I need Your strength... I am going to tell my accountability. I have to. Thank You.

Thank You for being a God of justice. I find myself keeping a list of all the people that have hurt me, like Kelly, and I imagine revenge, but God, "No acts of injustice escape Your notice." Please heal me. I want to feel light and free again. Help me to release her today, so I can see her and not give in to frustration. Help me to trust again. I surrender Lord! I don't want to protect myself. I want to live in Your protection! I will memorize this scripture today, Lord. Your promises are so great! Thank You for Jesus! I want to live in His freedom. Be with me today!

"It is my prayer that the promises of God for wholeness and freedom become your portion through this journal. May everything the enemy employed in the hope of taking you out be turned around to become a true testimony of the strength you possess when in the arms of your Maker, the One Who gave His all for you. May every day be filled with inspiration!"

January 1

In Noah's Ark

Genesis 7:1
Go into the ark, you and your whole family...
NIV

January 2

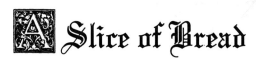

Slice of Bread

Deuteronomy 15:4
Save when there shall be no poor among you...
KJV

January 3

Satisfying Companionship

Psalm 25:14
*The secret [of the sweet, satisfying companionship] of the
Lord have they who fear Him,*
AMP

January 4

When You Wake

Psalm 17:15
As for me, I will continue beholding Your face in righteousness, I
shall be fully satisfied when I awake, beholding Your countenance.
Author's Paraphrase

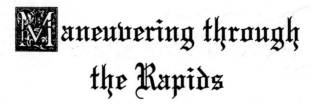

Maneuvering through the Rapids

Psalm 107:29
He hushes the storm to a calm and to a gentle whisper, so that the waves of the sea are still.
AMP

January 6

True Escape

2 Timothy 2:26
They will escape out of the snare of the devil and do the will of God.
Author's Paraphrase

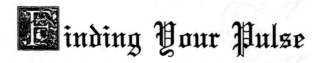inding Your Pulse

Matthew 6:21
For where your treasure is, there will your heart be also.
KJV

January 8

Acts 3:7
And He took him by the right hand, and lifted him up: and
immediately his feet and ankles bones received strength.
KJV

January 9

Act Like Clay

Isaiah 64:8
We are the clay, and You our potter; and
we are the work of Your hand.
NKJV

January 10

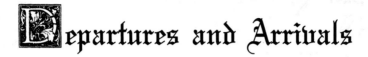

Departures and Arrivals

Deuteronomy 28:6
Blessed shalt thou be when thou comest in, and
blessed shalt thou be when thou goest out.
KJV

January 11

Learned Contentment

Philippians 4:11
For I have learned how to be content in whatever state I am.
Author's Paraphrase

January 12

The Gift of Thirst

Psalm 42:2
My inner self thirsts for God, for the living God.
When shall I come and behold the face of God?
AMP

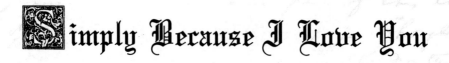

Simply Because I Love You

Proverbs 15:6
In the house of the righteous there is much treasure: but in
the revenue of the wicked is trouble.
KJV

January 14

I Am Listening

1 John 5:14
And this is the confidence which we have in Him: that if we ask
anything according to His will, He listens to and hears us.
AMP

January 15

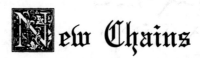

New Chains

Jeremiah 40:4
And now, behold, I loose thee this day from the chains
which were upon thine hand...
KJV

The Key to My House

Hebrews 4:16
Come boldly to the throne of grace, that we may obtain
mercy and find grace to help in time of need.
NKJV

nstoppable

Acts 5:39
But if it be of God, ye cannot overthrow it...
KJV

January 18

The Sound of a Growing Heart

Philippians 2:13
For it is God which worketh in you both to
will and to do of his good pleasure.
KJV

In the Quiet Place

1 Chronicles 4:40
And they found fat pasture and good, and the land
was wide, and quiet, and peaceable.
KJV

Branches of Your Will

Matthew 26:39

And he went a little farther, and fell on his face, and prayed, saying,
O my Father, if it be possible, let this cup pass from me:
nevertheless not as I will, but as thou wilt.
KJV

January 21

All the Pieces of You

Psalm 139:16
*Thine eyes did see my substance, yet being unperfect; and in thy
book all my members were written, which in continuance were fash-
ioned, when as yet there was none of them.*
KJV

January 22

I Offer You Me

Jeremiah 31:3
The Lord hath appeared of old unto me, saying,
Yea, I have loved thee with an everlasting love: therefore with
lovingkindness have I drawn thee.
KJV

The Sand Under Your Feet

Matthew 7:24
Therefore whosoever heareth these sayings of mine, and doeth them, I will liken him unto a wise man, which built his house upon a rock.
KJV

January 24

I Am Passing By

Matthew 9:22
Daughter, be of good comfort; thy faith hath made thee whole.
And the woman was made whole from that hour.
KJV

Burn

John 2:17
And His disciples remembered that it was written,
The zeal of thine house hath eaten me up.
KJV

Hungry Soul Moves Me

Matthew 5:6
Blessed are they which do hunger and thirst after
righteousness: for they shall be filled.
KJV

January 27

 Give All of Myself to You

Luke 5:20
Man, thy sins are forgiven thee.
KJV

January 28

Defeated Foes

Revelation 12:10
For the accuser of our brethren is cast down, which
accused them before our God day and night.
KJV

My Word Is Your Key

1 Samuel 9:27
But stand thou still a while, that I may
shew thee the word of God.
KJV

January 30

 **Let Me**

Revelation 3:20
Behold, I stand at the door, and knock: if any man
hear my voice, and open the door, I will come in to him, and
will sup with him, and he with me.
KJV

A New Heart

1 Samuel 10:6,9
The Spirit of the Lord came upon Saul and he stood up and turned around and God gave him another heart.
Author's Paraphrase

The Quiet Storm

Mark 4:39
And he arose, and rebuked the wind,
and said unto the sea, Peace, be still...
KJV

February 2

The Beholding

John 12:21
Sir, we would see Jesus.
KJV

My Hands

Matthew 8:3
Jesus put forth his hand and touched him and said, Be thou whole.
Author's Paraphrase

February 4

I Can See the Future

2 Corinthians 4:7
We possess this precious treasure in human vessels that
God's power may be seen in us, through us, and for us.
Author's Paraphrase

February 5

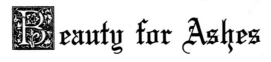

Beauty for Ashes

Isaiah 61:3
To console those who mourn in Zion,
To give them beauty for ashes...
NKJV

he Architect

1 Corinthians 3:9
For we are God's fellow workers; you are
God's field, you are God's building.
NKJV

February 7

Marked

2 Corinthians 9:8
And God is able to make all grace abound toward you,
that you, always having all sufficiency in all things, may
have an abundance for every good work.
NKJV

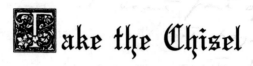ake the Chisel

John 15:3
You are already clean because of the word
which I have spoken to you.
NKJV

February 9

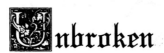nbroken

Luke 10:33
But a certain Samaritan, as he journeyed, came where he was.
And when he saw him, he had compassion.
NKJV

February 10

Unbroken Fellowship

1 John 1:7
If you walk in the Light of My truth as I am in the Light,
we have unbroken fellowship with one another, and the blood of
Jesus Christ cleanses you from all sin and guilt.
Author's Paraphrase

February 11

Giving Yourself

Isaiah 58:10
And if you give yourself to the hungry and satisfy
the desire of the afflicted, then your light will rise in
darkness and your gloom will become like midday.
NASB

February 12

The Root Ax

Psalm 145:14-15
The Lord upholdeth all that fall, and raiseth up all
those that be bowed down. The eyes of all wait upon thee;
and thou givest them their meat in due season.
KJV

 My Welcomed Guest

Psalm 121:7-8
He keeps you from all evil and preserves your life. He keeps
his eye upon you as you come and go, and always guards you.
TLB

February 14

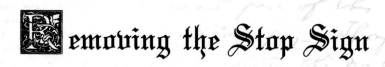

Removing the Stop Sign

Isaiah 40:2
Your warfare is over, your iniquity is cleansed, you
will receive a double portion of joy for all of your misery.
Author's Paraphrase

February 15

Watching Over You

Isaiah 49:10
They shall neither hunger nor thirst; the searing sun and
scorching desert winds will not reach them any more. For
the Lord in his mercy will lead them beside the cool waters.
TLB

February 16

Out of the Lion's Mouth

Amos 3:12
I will take you out of the mouth of the lion, piece by
piece, and heal the wounds of the predator's teeth.
Author's Paraphrase

ome to My House

Luke 8:41
*And behold, there came a man named Jairus, and he
was a ruler of the synagogue. And he fell down at Jesus' feet and
begged Him to come to his house.*
NKJV

ecoming Clay

Jeremiah 18:6
Look, as the clay is in the potter's hand,
so are you in My hand...
NKJV

The Watchman's Trumpet

Ezekiel 33:6
But if the watchman sees the sword coming and does not blow the trumpet, and the people are not warned, and the sword comes and takes any person from among them, he is taken away in his iniquity; but his blood I will require at the watchman's hand.
NKJV

February 20

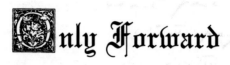

Only Forward

Exodus 14:15
The Lord said to Moses, "Why do you cry to me?
Tell the people of Israel to go forward.
ESV

February 21

With Open Hands

Matthew 13:8
But others fell on good ground and yielded a crop:
some a hundredfold, some sixty, some thirty.
NKJV

February 22

Feasting on Me

Psalm 107:9
*For He satisfieth the longing soul, and filleth
the hungry soul with goodness.*
KJV

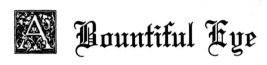

Bountiful Eye

Proverbs 22:9
He that hath a bountiful eye shall be blessed;
for he giveth of his bread to the poor.
KJV

February 24

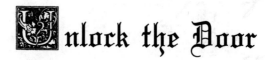

Unlock the Door

Luke 16:10-11
He that is faithful in that which is least is faithful also in much: and he that is unjust in the least is unjust also in much. If therefore ye have not been faithful in the unrighteous mammon, who will commit to your trust the true riches?
KJV

February 25

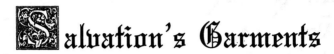

Salvation's Garments

Isaiah 61:10
I will greatly rejoice in the Lord; my soul shall exult in my God, for He has clothed me with the garments of salvation; He has covered me with the robe of righteousness.
ESV

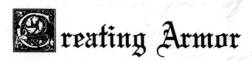reating Armor

Colossians 4:6
*Let your speech at all times be gracious (pleasant
and winsome), seasoned [as it were] with salt, [so that
you may never be at a loss] to know how you ought to
answer anyone [who puts a question to you].*
AMP

The Fields Are Waking Up

1 Kings 18:41
Then Elijah said to Ahab, "Go up, eat and drink; for
there is the sound of abundance of rain."
NKJV

 repared Triumphs

Proverbs 12:11
He who tills his land shall be satisfied with bread, but he who
follows worthless pursuits is lacking in sense and is without
understanding.
AMP

Formed in the Hands of Love

Isaiah 64:8
But now, I am your Father; you are the clay, and I am
your Potter; and you are the work of My hand.
Author's Paraphrase

Stay in the Garden

Genesis 3:8
*And they heard the voice of the Lord God
walking in the garden in the cool of the day...*
KJV

urden-free Living

Psalm 55:22
Cast thy burden upon the Lord, and He shall sustain thee:
He shall never suffer the righteous to be moved.
KJV

Pull Up Your Anchor

1 Peter 2:9
But you are a chosen race, a royal priesthood, a holy nation, a people for his own possession, that you may proclaim the excellencies of Him who called you out of darkness into his marvelous light.
ESV

Your Past Is Forgotten

2 Corinthians 5:17
Therefore, if anyone is in Christ, he is a new creation.
The old has passed away; behold, the new has come.
ESV

Take My Coat

1 Corinthians 13:7
Love bears up under anything and everything that comes, is ever ready to believe the best of every person, its hopes are fadeless under all circumstances, and it endures everything [without weakening].
AMP

March 6

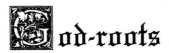

God-roots

Ephesians 3:16
That He would grant you, according to the riches of His glory, to be
strengthened with might through His Spirit in the inner man.
NKJV

March 7

Unhindered

Psalm 27:1-2

The Lord is my light and my salvation; whom shall I fear? The Lord is the strength of my life; of whom shall I be afraid? When the wicked, even mine enemies and my foes, came upon me to eat up my flesh, they stumbled and fell.
KJV

March 8

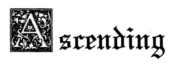

Ascending

Psalm 15:1
Lord, who shall abide in thy tabernacle? Who shall dwell in thy
holy hill?
KJV

March 9

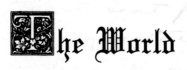

The World

1 John 2:15
Do not love the world or the things in the world. If anyone loves the world, the love of the Father is not in him.
ESV

Your Portion

Proverbs 12:7
The wicked are overthrown and are not, but the house
of the [uncompromisingly] righteous shall stand.
AMP

March 11

Completely Soaked

Zechariah 10:1
Ask ye of the Lord rain in the time of the
latter rain; so the Lord shall make bright
clouds, and give them showers of rain,
to every one grass in the field.
KJV

The Embrace of Brokenness

Luke 22:19
And he took bread, and gave thanks, and brake it,
and gave unto them, saying, This is My body which is given
for you: this do in remembrance of me.
KJV

March 13

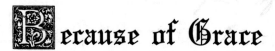

Because of Grace

1 Corinthians 15:10
But by the grace of God I am what I am, and his grace to me
was not without effect. No, I worked harder than all of them - yet
not I, but the grace of God that was with me.
NIV

Am Your Windmill

Psalm 115:14
The Lord shall increase you more and
more, you and your children.
KJV

March 15

Out of Darkness

Colossians 1:13
*Who hath delivered us from the power of darkness, and
hath translated us into the kingdom of his dear Son.*
KJV

Winged Seeds

Genesis 8:22
While the earth remaineth, seedtime
and harvest, and cold and heat, and summer and winter,
and day and night shall not cease.
KJV

asted Days Reclaimed

Romans 13:12
The night is far spent, the day is at hand: let us therefore cast off the works of darkness, and let us put on the armour of light.
KJV

March 18

Unlimited Power

Luke 4:14
There Jesus returned in the unlimited power of the
spirit – and his fame spread through the whole region.
Author's Paraphrase

March 19

Under My Care

Psalm 121:7-8
He keeps you from all evil and preserves your life. He keeps
his eye upon you as you come and go and always guards you.
Author's Paraphrase.

March 20

With Me

Genesis 39:2
The Lord was with Joseph in everything he did.
Author's Paraphrase

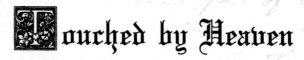

Touched by Heaven

Acts 4:13
When they saw the boldness and unfettered eloquence of
Peter and John and perceived they were unlearned, they marveled
and knew they had been with Jesus.
Author's Paraphrase

These Nailed, Pierced Hands

Luke 24:39
Behold my hands and my feet, that it is I
myself: handle me, and see; for a spirit hath not flesh
and bones, as ye see me have.
KJV

The Riches of Grace

Hebrews 4:16
Draw near to My throne of grace with boldness, that you may
receive mercy and find grace to help you in your time of need.
Author's Paraphrase

The Homeless Seed

Ecclesiastes 11:1
Cast your seed upon the waters, you will find it after many days.
Author's Paraphrase

The Heart

Ezekiel 11:19
And I will give them one heart, a soft heart, and I will put a
new spirit within them, and I will remove the stony heart, and give
them a heart easily moved by my spirit.
Author's Paraphrase

March 26

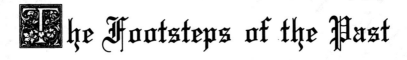

The Footsteps of the Past

Exodus 14:13
The Egyptians which have pursued you and
tormented you will you see no more.
Author's Paraphrase

_____
_____
_____
_____
_____
_____
_____
_____
_____
_____
_____
_____
_____
_____
_____
_____
_____
_____
_____

March 27

The Buttered Road

Job 29:6
Your steps were washed in butter and the
rock poured out rivers of oil.
Author's Paraphrase.

March 28

 oyalty

Proverbs 10:22
The blessing of the Lord, it maketh rich, and
he addeth no sorrow with it.
KJV

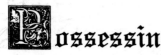ossessing the Enemy's Gate

Genesis 22:17
...And your seed will possess the gates of your enemies.
Author's Paraphrase

March 30

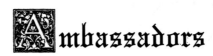 **Ambassadors**

2 Corinthians 5:20
Now then we are ambassadors for Christ, as though
God did beseech you by us: we pray you in Christ's
stead, be ye reconciled to God.
KJV

Of Hammered Gold

1 Peter 1:7
That the trial of your faith, being much more
precious than of gold that perisheth, though it be tried
with fire, might be found unto praise and honour and glory
at the appearing of Jesus Christ.
KJV

April 1

Love's Breath

Ephesians 5:2
And walk in love, as Christ also hath loved us,
and hath given himself for us an offering and a
sacrifice to God for a sweetsmelling savour.
KJV

April 2

Life Injections

2 Thessalonians 2:17
May the Lord strengthen, comfort, and make you
steadfast and unmovable in every good work and word.
Author's Paraphrase

ngel Armor

Jeremiah 1:18
I have made you a protected city and an iron
pillar and brazen walls – none can harm you.
Author's Paraphrase

 limbing Down

Micah 6:8
He hath shewed thee, O man, what is good; and what doth the Lord require of thee, but to do justly, and to love mercy, and to walk humbly with thy God?
KJV

Dreamers Never Die

Joel 2:28
And it shall come to pass afterward, that I will
pour out my spirit upon all flesh; and your sons
and your daughters shall prophesy, your old men shall
dream dreams, your young men shall see visions.
KJV

April 6

Enduring

James 5:11
Behold, we count them happy which endure...
KJV

April 7

Finding Your Harp

Psalm 137:2
We hung our harps by the willow trees.
Author's Paraphrase

Give Me Your Ear, Fastened to the Door

Exodus 21:6
Then his master shall bring him unto the judges; he shall also bring him to the door, or unto the door post; and his master shall bore his ear through with an aul; and he shall serve him for ever.
KJV

April 9

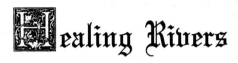

Healing Rivers

John 7:38
He that believeth on me, out of his
belly shall flow rivers of living water.
Author's Paraphrase

April 10

I Am with You

Matthew 28:20
...I am with you always, even unto
the end of the world. Amen.
KJV

April 11

When Heaven Smiles

Numbers 6:24-26
The Lord bless you and keep you; the Lord make His
face shine upon you, And be gracious to you; the Lord lift
up His countenance upon you, and give you peace.
NKJV

April 12

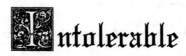ntolerable

Exodus 2:23
And it came to pass in process of time, that
the king of Egypt died: and the children of Israel
sighed by reason of the bondage, and they cried, and their
cry came up unto God by reason of the bondage.
KJV

April 13

1 John 5:14
And this is the confidence which we have in Him: that if we ask anything according to His will (in agreement with His own plan), He listens to and hears us.
AMP

April 14

It Is Spoken. It Is Written. It Is Done.

James 1:17
*Every good gift and every perfect gift is from above,
and cometh down from the Father of lights, with whom is no variableness, neither shadow of turning.*
KJV

April 15

You're Worth It

1 Thessalonians 5:24
Faithful is He that calleth you, who also will do it.
KJV

April 16

Four Things

Proverbs 22:29
Do you see a man diligent and skillful in his business?
He will stand before kings; he will not stand before obscure men.
AMP

April 17

Unbreakable

Psalm 89:34
*My covenant will I not break, nor alter the
thing that is gone out of my lips.*
KJV

April 18

nchangeable

Malachi 3:6
For I am the Lord, I change not; therefore
ye sons of Jacob are not consumed.
KJV

When the Clouds Roll Away

2 Timothy 2:21
If a man therefore purge himself from these,
he shall be a vessel unto honour, sanctified, and meet for the
master's use, and prepared unto every good work.
KJV

April 20

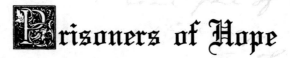

Prisoners of Hope

Zechariah 9:12
*Turn you to the strong hold, ye prisoners of hope: even
to day do I declare that I will render double unto thee.*
KJV

April 21

Keep Your Eyes Open

Numbers 13:30
And Caleb stilled the people before Moses,
and said, Let us go up at once, and possess it;
for we are well able to overcome it.
KJV

April 22

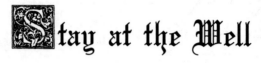 **Stay at the Well**

Psalm 139:17-18
*How precious also are thy thoughts unto me, O God! How great
is the sum of them! If I should count them, they are more in number
than the sand: when I awake, I am still with thee.*
KJV

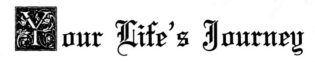our Life's Journey

Genesis 22:8
And Abraham said, My son, God
will provide himself a lamb for a burnt offering:
so they went both of them together.
KJV

April 24

The Unstoppable Hand

Daniel 4:35
*And all the inhabitants of the earth are reputed as nothing:
and he doeth according to his will in the army of heaven, and
among the inhabitants of the earth: and none can stay his
hand, or say unto him, What doest thou?*
KJV

April 25

roken Curses

Luke 10:19
Behold, I give unto you power to tread on serpents
and scorpions, and over all the power of the enemy:
and nothing shall by any means hurt you.
KJV

April 26

When Heaven Shouts

Isaiah 1:17
Learn to do well; seek
judgment, relieve the oppressed, judge the
fatherless, plead for the widow.
KJV

The Warehouse

Nehemiah 9:21
Forty years You sustained them in the
wilderness; they lacked nothing, their clothes did
not wear out, and their feet did not swell.
AMP

Twenty-four Hours a Day

1 Peter 1:5
Who are kept by the power of God through faith
unto salvation ready to be revealed in the last time.
KJV

The Prize

Philippians 3:14
I press on toward the goal to win the prize
to which God in Christ Jesus has called me to.
Author's Paraphrase

April 30

 verwhelmed

Joshua 3:15
Dip your feet in the garden, and the
waters will overflow its banks.
Author's Paraphrase

May 1

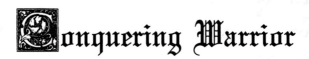

Conquering Warrior

Isaiah 14:3
I will lift your heavy load and give you rest from sorrow and fear.
You will know that all the mighty tyrants have been destroyed.
Author's Paraphrase

May 2

Double Your Strength

Numbers 11:17
And I will come down and talk with thee there: and
I will take of the spirit which is upon thee...
KJV

May 3

My Waiting Arms

Isaiah 52:7
How beautiful upon the mountains are the feet of him that bring-
eth good tidings, that publisheth peace; that bringeth good tidings
of good, that publisheth salvation; that saith unto Zion, Thy God
reigneth!
KJV

May 4

Sacred Place

Exodus 25:22
I will meet with you and commune with you from
between the wings of the cherubim from above the mercy seat and
reveal to you everything you need to know.
Author's Paraphrase

May 5

If I Speak

Isaiah 46:11
Yes, I have spoken, and I will bring it
to pass; I have purposed it, and I will do it.
AMP

May 6

The Unveiled Heart

Isaiah 33:16
[Such a man] will dwell on the heights;
his place of defense will be the fortresses of rocks; his bread will be
given him; water for him will be sure.
AMP

he Naked Heart

Joshua 3:5
...Sanctify yourselves: for tomorrow the Lord will do
wonders among you.
KJV

May 8

Unwind

Psalm 37:7
*Rest in the Lord, and wait patiently for
Him: fret not thyself because of him who prospereth
in his way, because of the man who bringeth
wicked devices to pass.*
KJV

May 9

My Divine Yes

Exodus 3:21
I will grant you favor in the sight of the Egyptians,
and it shall come to pass that when you go out,
you will not go out empty-handed.
Author's Paraphrase

May 10

Destroying Yokes

Isaiah 10:27
The burdens shall depart from off
your shoulders and the yokes from your neck.
Author's Paraphrase

_____

_____

_____

_____

_____

_____

_____

_____

_____

_____

_____

_____

May 11

Knees

Leviticus 10:7
Stay in the tent of meeting, lest you die:
for the Lord's anointing oil is upon you.
Author's Paraphrase

May 12

The -Ites

Joshua 3:10
I will drive out from your midst the Canaanites,
Hittites, Perizzites, Girgashites, Amorites, and the Jebusites.
Author's Paraphrase

May 13

Live in Reverse

Exodus 1:12
But the more they afflicted them, the
more they multiplied and grew...
NKJV

May 14

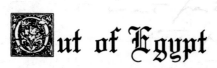

Out of Egypt

Deuteronomy 26:8
I brought you out of the house of bondage
with a mighty hand and with signs and wonders.
Author's Paraphrase

May 15

Fruit that Never Wastes

John 15:16
You did not choose Me, but I chose you and
appointed you that you should go and bear fruit,
and that your fruit should remain, that whatever you
ask the Father in My name He may give you.
NKJV

May 16

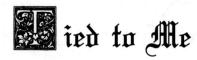

Tied to Me

Hosea 11:4
I drew you with cords of love and I removed
your yokes and bent down and laid food before you.
Author's Paraphrase

_____

_____

_____

_____

_____

_____

_____

_____

_____

_____

_____

_____

_____

May 17

The Inner Chamber

1 Samuel 19:2
...Abide in a secret place, and hide thyself.
KJV

May 18

The Kisses of Surrender

Song of Solomon 1:2
Let him kiss me with the kisses of his mouth:
for thy love is better than wine.
KJV

That Love Divine

Romans 5:8
But God commendeth His love toward us, in that,
while we were yet sinners, Christ died for us.
KJV

May 20

When I Come to Stay

Song of Solomon 2:16
My beloved is mine, and I am his...
NKJV

May 21

 Garden Called Loved

Song of Solomon 4:12
A garden enclosed is my sister...
NKJV

_____

_____

_____

_____

_____

_____

_____

_____

_____

_____

_____

_____

_____

_____

_____

_____

_____

Drink Deeply

Song of Solomon 5:1
Drink deeply my milk and wine and the honeycomb.
Author's Paraphrase

May 23

The Fabric of Eternity

Ecclesiastes 3:14
I know that, whatsoever God doeth, it shall be for ever:
nothing can be put to it, nor anything taken from it: and God
doeth it, that men should fear before him.
KJV

 Fully Persuaded

Romans 4:21
And being fully persuaded that, what he had
promised, he was able also to perform.
KJV

Became Poor

2 Corinthians 8:9
For ye know the grace of our Lord
Jesus Christ, that, though he was rich,
yet for your sakes he became poor, that
ye through his poverty might be rich.
KJV

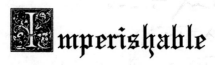mperishable

1 Peter 1:23
You have been born again not of perishable seed,
but of imperishable seed through the living and enduring Word of
God. Author's Paraphrase

The Tailored Life

Colossians 2:2
That their hearts might be comforted, being knit
together in love, and unto all riches of the full assurance of
understanding, to the acknowledgement of the mystery of God,
and of the Father, and of Christ.
KJV

My Name Is Beauty

Ecclesiastes 3:11
He has made everything beautiful in its
time. Also He has put eternity in their hearts...
NKJV

May 29

Live with Your Wings Spread

Psalm 37:5
Commit your way to the Lord [roll and
repose each care of your load on Him]; trust
also in Him and he will bring it to pass.
AMP

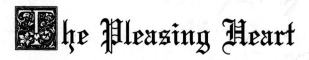The Pleasing Heart

Colossians 1:10
That you may walk worthy of the Lord,
fully pleasing Him, being fruitful in every good
work and increasing in the knowledge of God.
NKJV

Glowing

Romans 12:11
Never lag in zeal and in earnest endeavor; be aglow
and burning with the Spirit, serving the Lord.
AMP

June 1

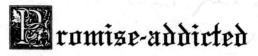

Promise-addicted

2 Peter 1:4
Whereby are given unto us exceeding
great and precious promises: that by these ye
might be partakers of the divine nature...
KJV

June 2

esigned

Ephesians 2:10
For we are God's handiwork, created in Christ Jesus
that we may do good works, that we should walk in them.
Author's Paraphrase

The Irresistible Blessing

Genesis 39:5
And it came to pass from the time that he had made him overseer in his house, and over all that he had, that the Lord blessed the Egyptian's house for Joseph's sake; and the blessing of the Lord was upon all that he had in the house, and in the field.
KJV

June 4

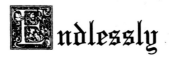

Endlessly

2 Chronicles 26:5
...And as long as he sought the Lord,
God made him to prosper.
KJV

June 5

In the Hollow of My Hand

Psalm 128:1-2
Blessed is every one that feareth the Lord; that walketh in his ways. For thou shalt eat the labour of thine hands: happy shalt thou be, and it shall be well with thee.
KJV

My Eyes

Luke 15:20
And he arose, and came to his father. But
when he was yet a great way off, his father
saw him, and had compassion, and ran, and fell
on his neck, and kissed him.
KJV

June 7

 Parade of Victory

2 Corinthians 2:14
Now thanks be unto God, which always causeth us
to triumph in Christ, and maketh manifest the
savour of his knowledge by us in every place.
KJV

June 8

 Sevenfold Day

Luke 7:50
And he said to the woman, Thy faith
hath saved thee; go in peace.
KJV

June 9

Before You Call, I Will Answer

Isaiah 65:24
*Before you call, I will answer
and while you are yet speaking, I will hear.*
Author's Paraphrase

June 10

Until You Look Like Me

2 Corinthians 3:18
But we all, with open face beholding as in a
glass the glory of the Lord, are changed into the
same image from glory to glory, even as by
the Spirit of the Lord.
KJV

June 11

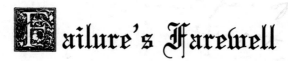

Failure's Farewell

Psalm 25:9-10
The meek will he guide in judgment: and the meek
will he teach his way. All the paths of the Lord are mercy and truth
unto such as keep his covenant and his testimonies.
KJV

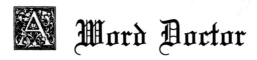

Word Doctor

Luke 21:15
For I will give you a mouth and wisdom, which
all your adversaries shall not be able to gainsay nor resist.
KJV

June 13

Till the Very End

John 13:1
Jesus knew his time had come and he
loved his own till the very end.
Author's Paraphrase

June 14

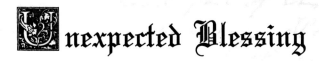

Unexpected Blessing

Psalm 119:9
Wherewithal shall a young man cleanse his way?
by taking heed thereto according to thy word.
KJV

June 15

The Trusting Soul

Psalm 37:39
But the salvation of the righteous is of the Lord:
he is their strength in the time of trouble.
KJV

 When Your Barns Are Full

Proverbs 3:10
So shall thy barns be filled with plenty, and
thy presses shall burst out with new wine.
KJV

Living in Full View

Ephesians 1:18
The eyes of your understanding being enlightened;
that ye may know what is the hope of his calling...
KJV

Spiritual Immunity

Isaiah 54:17
No weapon that is formed against thee shall
prosper; and every tongue that shall rise against
thee in judgment thou shalt condemn...
KJV

June 19

othing Is Too Difficult

Jeremiah 32:17
Ah Lord God! ...there is nothing too hard for thee.
KJV

_____

_____

_____

_____

_____

_____

_____

_____

_____

_____

_____

_____

_____

_____

_____

_____

_____

_____

June 20

Even Deserts Are My Opportunities

Isaiah 51:3
For the Lord comforts Zion; he comforts all her
waste places and makes her wilderness like Eden, her desert
like the garden of the Lord; joy and gladness will be found in her,
thanksgiving and the voice of song.
ESV

June 21

Exodus 33:14-15
And he said, My presence shall go with thee, and
I will give thee rest. And he said unto him, If thy presence go not
with me, carry us not up hence.
KJV

June 22

The Healing Spring

Psalm 52:8
But I am like a green olive tree in the house of God:
I trust in the mercy of God for ever and ever.
KJV

The Tattered Coat

Genesis 37:3
Now Israel loved Joseph more than all
his children, because he was the son of his old age:
and he made him a coat of many colours.
KJV

June 24

Never Doubt

Psalm 23:5
Thou preparest a table before me in the presence of mine enemies: thou anointest my head with oil; my cup runneth over.
KJV

June 25

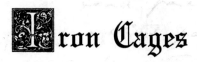

Iron Cages

Isaiah 45:2
I will go before thee, and make the crooked
places straight: I will break in pieces the gates of brass,
and cut in sunder the bars of iron.
KJV

ith Every Cell

Romans 5:8
But God commendeth his love toward us, in that,
while we were yet sinners, Christ died for us.
KJV

 The Thieves' Den

Proverbs 6:30
Men do not despise a thief, if he steal to
satisfy his soul when he is hungry.
KJV

June 28

 Significant Life

Psalm 37:23
The steps of a good man are ordered by the Lord:
and he delighteth in his way.
KJV

June 29

The Green Light

Isaiah 56:5
...I will give them an everlasting name,
that shall not be cut off.
KJV

Protection's Name

Isaiah 41:10
Fear thou not; for I am with thee: be not dismayed;
for I am thy God: I will strengthen thee; yea, I will
help thee; yea, I will uphold thee with the
right hand of my righteousness.
KJV

July 1

he Narrow Road

Matthew 7:13-14

Enter ye in at the strait gate: for wide is the gate, and broad is the way, that leadeth to destruction, and many there be which go in thereat.

KJV

July 2

 Guarded Garden

Song of Solomon 4:12
A garden inclosed is my sister, my spouse;
a spring shut up, a fountain sealed.
KJV

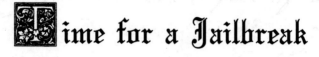ime for a Jailbreak

Acts 16:26
And suddenly there was a great earthquake,
so that the foundations of the prison were shaken:
and immediately all the doors were opened, and
every one's bands were loosed.
KJV

July 4

But Me

Psalm 139:1-2
O Lord, thou hast searched me, and known me. Thou knowest my
downsitting and mine uprising, thou understandest my thought afar
off. KJV

July 5

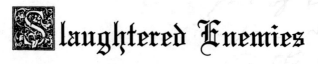

Slaughtered Enemies

Psalm 41:11
*By this I know that thou favourest me, because
mine enemy doth not triumph over me.*
KJV

July 6

Rat Catchers

Psalm 141:10
Let the wicked fall into their own nets,
whilst that I withal escape.
KJV

July 7

Divine Outbreaks

Mark 2:2
And straightway many were gathered together,
insomuch that there was no room to receive them,
no, not so much as about the door: and he
preached the word unto them.
KJV

July 8

The Anchor Smith

Hebrews 6:18
That by two immutable things, in which it was
impossible for God to lie, we might have a strong
consolation, who have fled for refuge to lay hold
upon the hope set before us.
KJV

July 9

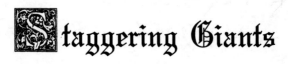

Staggering Giants

Psalm 18:17
He delivered me from my strong enemy, and from
them which hated me: for they were too strong for me.
KJV

_____
_____
_____
_____
_____
_____
_____
_____
_____
_____
_____
_____
_____
_____
_____
_____
_____

July 10

 ## Bag of Magic Tricks

2 Corinthians 1:1
Paul, an apostle of Jesus Christ by the will of God, and
Timothy our brother, unto the church of God which is at Corinth,
with all the saints which are in all Achaia.
KJV

July 11

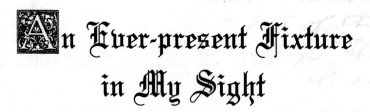

An Ever-present Fixture
in My Sight

Daniel 4:35
And all the inhabitants of the earth are reputed as nothing:
and he doeth according to his will in the army of heaven,
and among the inhabitants of the earth: and none can stay his hand,
or say unto him, What doest thou?
KJV

July 12

Time Is Ticking

Ephesians 5:16
Redeeming the time, because the days are evil.
KJV

July 13

arry Your Medicine with You

Isaiah 53:3
He is despised and rejected of men; a man of sorrows,
and acquainted with grief: and we hid as it were our faces from him;
he was despised, and we esteemed him not.
KJV

July 14

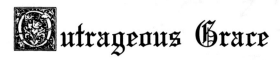

Outrageous Grace

2 Corinthians 9:8
And God is able to make all grace abound toward you; that ye, always having all sufficiency in all things, may abound to every good work. KJV

July 15

Philippians 4:19
But my God shall supply all your need
according to his riches in glory by Christ Jesus.
KJV

_____

_____

_____

_____

_____

_____

_____

_____

_____

_____

_____

_____

July 16

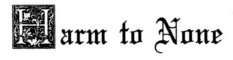

Harm to None

Matthew 10:6
But go rather to the lost sheep of the house of Israel.
KJV

July 17

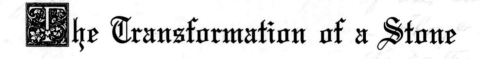

The Transformation of a Stone

Ephesians 4:32
And be ye kind one to another, tenderhearted, forgiving
one another, even as God for Christ's sake hath forgiven you.
KJV

The Hungry Heart

Matthew 5:8
Blessed are the pure in heart: for they shall see God.
KJV

Handmade

Psalm 139:14
I will praise thee; for I am fearfully and wonderfully made:
marvelous are thy works; and that my soul knoweth right well.
KJV

he Miry Clay

Psalm 40:2
He brought me up also out of an horrible pit, out of
the miry clay, and set my feet upon a rock, and established my go-
ings. KJV

Where Are Your Stretch Marks?

Matthew 14:26
And when the disciples saw him walking
on the sea, they were troubled, saying, It is a
spirit; and they cried out for fear.
KJV

July 22

The Key Master

Revelation 3:8
I know thy works: behold, I have set before thee an open
door, and no man can shut it: for thou hast a little strength, and
hast kept my word, and hast not denied my name.
KJV

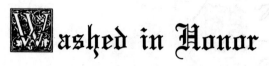ashed in Honor

1 Peter 2:17
Honour all men...
KJV

July 24

Evicting Slavery

Psalm 142:7
Bring my soul out of prison, that I may praise thy name: the right-
eous shall compass me about; for thou shalt deal bountifully with
me.
KJV

July 25

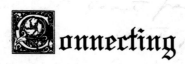
onnecting

1 Corinthians 1:10
...Be perfectly joined together in the
same mind and in the same judgment.
KJV

July 26

The Disease of Later

Proverbs 10:4
He becometh poor that dealeth with a slack hand:
but the hand of the diligent maketh rich.
KJV

Into the House

1 Peter 2:5
Ye also, as living stones, are built up as a spiritual
house, an holy priesthood, to offer up spiritual sacrifices,
acceptable to God by Jesus Christ.
KJV

July 28

The Purchaser

1 Corinthians 6:20
For ye are bought with a price: therefore glorify
God in your body, and in your spirit, which are God's.
KJV

July 29

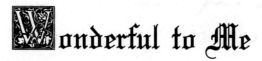

Wonderful to Me

Jeremiah 31:3
...I have loved thee with an everlasting love:
therefore with lovingkindness have I drawn thee.
KJV

July 30

 Sacred Words

Psalm 19:14
Let the words of my mouth, and the meditation of my heart, be acceptable in thy sight, O Lord, my strength, and my redeemer.
KJV

July 31

Entirely Mine

Psalm 139:13
*For thou hast possessed my reins: thou hast
covered me in my mother's womb.*
KJV

Debt Destroyer

Romans 13:8
Owe no man any thing, but to love one another:
for he that loveth another hath fulfilled the law.
KJV

_____
_____
_____
_____
_____
_____
_____
_____
_____
_____
_____
_____
_____

August 2

Without Fear

Deuteronomy 1:21
Behold, the Lord thy God hath set the land before thee:
go up and possess it, as the Lord God of thy fathers hath said unto
thee; fear not, neither be discouraged.
KJV

The World Changed

Ecclesiastes 3:11
He hath made every thing beautiful in his time: also he
hath set the world in their heart, so that no man can find out the
work that God maketh from the beginning to the end.
KJV

August 4

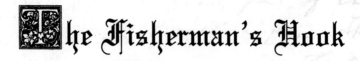

The Fisherman's Hook

Ezekiel 47:10

*...They shall be a place to spread forth nets; their fish shall
be according to their kinds, as the fish of the great sea,
exceeding many.*
KJV

_____
_____
_____
_____
_____
_____
_____
_____
_____
_____
_____
_____
_____
_____

Take This Hammer

2 Corinthians 6:16
And what agreement hath the temple of God with idols? for ye are
the temple of the living god; as God hath said, I will dwell in them,
and walk in them; and I will be their God,
and they shall be my people.
KJV

August 6

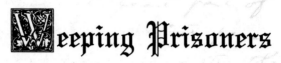

Weeping Prisoners

Isaiah 25:8
He will swallow up death in victory; and the Lord God will
wipe away tears from off all faces; and the rebuke of his people
shall he take away from off all the earth: for the
Lord hath spoken it.
KJV

August 7

 Am Looking

John 15:8
Herein is my Father glorified, that ye bear much
fruit; so shall ye be my disciples.
KJV

August 8

On the Road to Heaven

Matthew 22:9
*Go ye therefore into the highways, and as many
as ye shall find, bid to the marriage.*
KJV

The Freedom's Yoke

Matthew 11:28-29
Come unto me, all ye that labour and are heavy laden,
and I will give you rest. Take my yoke upon you, and
learn of me; for I am meek and lowly in heart: and ye
shall find rest unto your souls.
KJV

The Devil's Pen

2 Corinthians 10:5
Casting down imaginations, and every high thing
that exalteth itself against the knowledge of God, and
bringing into captivity every thought to the
obedience of Christ.
KJV

August 11

Building You

Ephesians 2:10
For we are his workmanship, created in
Christ Jesus unto good works, which God hath before ordained
that we should walk in them.
KJV

August 12

Aiming for the Stars

Psalm 57:7
My heart is fixed, O God, my heart is fixed:
I will sing and give praise.
KJV

he Gift

Joel 2:19
...Look, listen--I'm sending a gift:
Grain and wine and olive oil...
The Message Bible

August 14

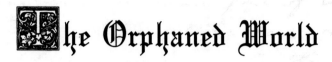

The Orphaned World

Hosea 14:3
For it is only in You that the fatherless can find mercy.
Author's Paraphrase

_____
_____
_____
_____
_____
_____
_____
_____
_____
_____
_____
_____
_____
_____

August 15

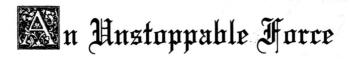

An Unstoppable Force

John 12:24
...Except a corn of wheat fall into
the ground and die, it abideth alone: but if it die,
it bringeth forth much fruit.
KJV

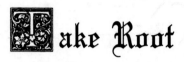

Take Root

Hosea 14:5
I will refresh Israel like the dew from heaven; he will
blossom as the lily and take root deeply in the
soil like cedars in Lebanon.
Author's Paraphrase

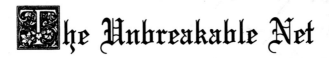

August 17

The Unbreakable Net

Matthew 4:19
...Follow Me, and I will make you fishers of men.
KJV

August 18

The Heart Lamp

Isaiah 60:2
...the Lord shall arise upon thee, and his glory
shall be seen upon thee.
KJV

August 19

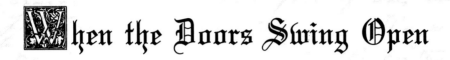

When the Doors Swing Open

1 Corinthians 16:9
For a great door and effectual is opened unto
me, and there are many adversaries.
KJV

Trusting

Psalm 125:1-2
They that trust in the Lord shall be as mount Zion, which cannot be removed, but abideth for ever. As the mountains are round about Jerusalem, so the Lord is round about his people from henceforth even for ever.
KJV

nshakable Foundations

Luke 14:28
For which of you, intending to build a tower,
sitteth not down first, and counteth the cost, whether
he have sufficient to finish it?
KJV

August 22

I Have No Trash Can

Isaiah 48:21
They did not thirst when he led them through
the deserts; he made water flow for them from the rock...
NIV

The Dance of Life

2 Samuel 6:14
David, wearing a linen ephod, danced before
the Lord with all his might.
NIV

August 24

All Grow Rich

Proverbs 31:7
*Let them drink and forget their poverty and
remember their misery no more.*
NIV

Your Character Paints Your Portrait

Matthew 5:16
Let your good works be seen by all men.
Author's Paraphrase

August 26

Never Abandoned

Hebrews 13:5
*Let your conversation be without covetousness;
and be content with such things as ye have: for he hath said, I
will never leave thee, nor forsake thee.*
KJV

August 27

Obtaining

1 Corinthians 9:24
Know ye not that they which run in a race run
all, but one receiveth the prize? So run, that ye may obtain.
KJV

August 28

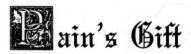

Pain's Gift

Psalm 94:19
In the multitude of my thoughts within me thy
comforts delight my soul.
KJV

August 29

Melted Down

Isaiah 48:10
Behold, I have refined thee, but not with
silver; I have chosen thee in the furnace of affliction.
KJV

August 30

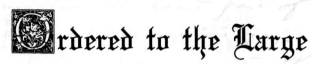

Ordered to the Large

Psalm 18:19
He brought me forth also into a large place;
he delivered me, because he delighted in me.
KJV

August 31

Stand Still

Exodus 14:13
And Moses said unto the people, Fear ye not,
stand still, and see the salvation of the Lord,
which he will shew to you to day...
KJV

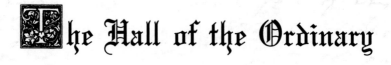

The Hall of the Ordinary

Psalm 33:12
Blessed is the nation whose God is the Lord: and
the people whom he hath chosen for his own inheritance.
KJV

September 2

Let Me Look Within

Psalm 139:23
Search me, O God, and know my heart:
try me, and know my thoughts.
KJV

Shielded

2 Timothy 2:26
*And that they may recover
themselves out of the snare of the devil, who are
taken captive by him at his will.*
KJV

 A Dove Sent Forth

Genesis 8:8
*Also he sent forth a dove from him, to see if the
waters were abated from off the face of the ground.
KJV*

September 5

 Give You a Wise Heart

Proverbs 16:21
The wise in heart are called prudent, understanding,
and knowing, and winsome speech increases learning.
AMP

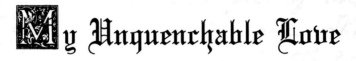

My Unquenchable Love

Song of Solomon 8:7
Many waters cannot quench love, neither
can floods drown it. If a man would offer all the goods of his
house for love, he would be utterly scorned and despised.
AMP

The Good News Highway

Psalm 112:7
*He shall not be afraid of evil tidings; his heart
is firmly fixed, trusting in the Lord.*
AMP

The Feet of a Warrior

Habakkuk 3:19
The Lord God is my Strength, my personal bravery,
and my invincible army; He makes my feet like hinds' feet and
will make me to walk and make [spiritual] progress upon my
high places [of trouble, suffering, or responsibility]!
AMP

September 9

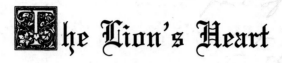

The Lion's Heart

Job 8:7
And though your beginning was small, yet your
latter end would greatly increase.
AMP

September 10

Live without Panic

Luke 24:36
Now while they were talking about this,
Jesus Himself took His stand among them and
said to them, Peace (freedom from all the distresses that
are experienced as the result of sin) be to you!
AMP

September 11

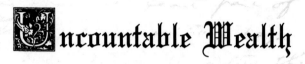
Uncountable Wealth

Ephesians 1:3
*Blessed be the God and Father of our Lord
Jesus Christ, who hath blessed us with all spiritual
blessings in heavenly places in Christ.*
KJV

September 12

Live Crucified, Walk Sanctified

Galatians 2:20

I am crucified with Christ: nevertheless I live; yet not I, but Christ liveth in me: and the life which I now live in the flesh I live by the faith of the Son of God, who loved me, and gave himself for me.
KJV

September 13

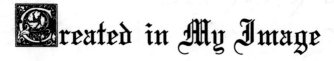

Created in My Image

Genesis 5:1
When God created man, He made
him in the likeness of God.
AMP

September 14

Take the Key from My Hand

Colossians 2:2-3

That their hearts might be comforted, being knit
together in love, and unto all riches of the full assurance of under-
standing, to the acknowledgement of the mystery of God,
and of the Father, and of Christ; In whom are hid
all the treasures of wisdom and knowledge.
KJV

 Polish Your Trophies of Grace

Ecclesiastes 3:11
He has made everything beautiful
in its time. He also has planted eternity in
men's hearts and minds...
AMP

September 16

Sing Your Way to Me

1 Chronicles 16:9
Sing to Him, sing psalms to Him;
Talk of all His wondrous works!
NKJV

September 17

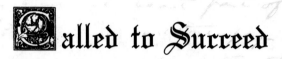Called to Succeed

Proverbs 16:3
Roll your works upon the Lord
[commit and trust them wholly to Him; He will
cause your thoughts to become agreeable to His will,
and] so shall your plans be established and succeed.
AMP

September 18

There Are Places

Colossians 1:9
...[asking] that you may be filled with the full
knowledge of His will in all spiritual wisdom and in
understanding and discernment of spiritual things.
AMP

September 19

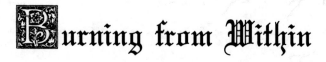

Burning from Within

Romans 12:11
Never lag in zeal and in earnest endeavor;
be aglow and burning with the Spirit, serving the Lord.
AMP

September 20

The Secret Sounds of Love

1 John 4:4
You, dear children, are from God and have overcome them,
because the one who is in you is greater
than the one who is in the world.
NIV

The Sound of My Plow

Ephesians 2:10
For we are God's handiwork (His workmanship),
recreated in Christ Jesus, that we may do those good works
which God predestined for us, that we should walk in them.
AMP

September 22

weet Communion

Psalm 25:14
The secret [of the sweet, satisfying companionship]
of the Lord have they who fear Him, and He will show them
His covenant and reveal to them its meaning.
AMP

September 23

In My Shoes

Matthew 3:11
*...but He who is coming after me is mightier than I, and
I am not fit to remove His sandals.*
NASB

September 24

The Heart Surgeon

Ezekiel 11:19
*And I will give them one heart and I will put a
new spirit within them; and I will take the stony heart out
of their flesh, and will give them a heart of flesh.
AMP*

The Power Source

2 Corinthians 13:4
For though he was crucified through weakness,
yet he liveth by the power of God. For we also are weak in him,
but we shall live with him by the power of God toward you.
KJV

Am What You Need

Psalm 16:5-6
The Lord is the portion of mine
inheritance and of my cup...
KJV

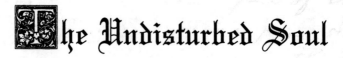The Undisturbed Soul

Philippians 4:11
I have learned how to be content
(satisfied to the point where I am not disturbed
or disquieted) in whatever state I am.
AMP

Drinker of Life

John 7:37
If any man thirst, let him come unto me and
drink and I will quench his thirst.
Author's Paraphrase

aptured by Heaven's Smile

Numbers 6:24-26
The Lord bless you and keep you; the Lord make
His face shine upon you, and be gracious to you; the Lord
lift up His countenance upon you, and give you peace.
NKJV

September 30

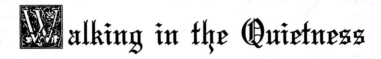

Walking in the Quietness

Psalm 15:2
He that walketh uprightly, and worketh
righteousness, and speaketh the truth in his heart.
KJV

October 1

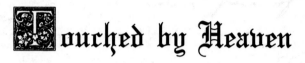

Touched by Heaven

Acts 4:13
Now when they saw the boldness and unfettered
eloquence of Peter and John and perceived that they were
unlearned and untrained in the schools, they marveled; and
they recognized that they had been with Jesus.
AMP

October 2

The Untouchable Soul

Daniel 1:8
But Daniel purposed in his heart that he would not
defile himself with the portion of the king's meat, nor with
the wine which he drank: therefore he requested of the prince
of the eunuchs that he might not defile himself.
KJV

Hidden

Psalm 31:20
*Thou shalt hide them in the secret of thy presence
from critical tongues: thou shalt keep them secretly in a pavilion
from the conspiracies of unscrupulous men.*
Author's Paraphrase

October 4

Not a Second Time

Nahum 1:9
Trust Me, says the Lord. This affliction shall
not rise up the second time.
Author's Paraphrase

October 5

ecoming a Masterpiece

2 Chronicles 16:9
*For the eyes of the Lord run to and fro
throughout the whole earth, to shew himself strong in the
behalf of them whose heart is perfect toward him...*
KJV

October 6

The Winter Is Over

Song of Solomon 2:11-12
For, lo, the winter is past, the rain
is over and gone; The flowers appear on the earth; the
time of the singing of birds is come...
KJV

October 7

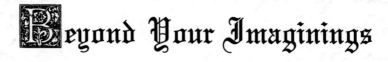eyond Your Imaginings

1 Corinthians 2:9
What eye has not seen and ear has not
heard and has not entered into the heart of man, [all
that] God has prepared for those who love Him.
AMP

October 8

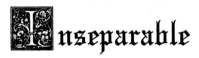

Inseparable

Romans 8:38-39
For I am convinced that neither death nor life, neither angels nor demons, neither the present nor the future, nor any powers, neither height nor depth, nor anything else in all creation, will be able to separate us from the love of God that is in Christ Jesus our Lord.
NIV

October 9

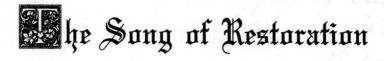

The Song of Restoration

Psalm 68:19
...The Lord who daily bears our
burdens and lifts our discouraging loads.
Author's Paraphrase

The Drought Is Over

1 Kings 18:41
And Elijah said to Ahab, Go up, eat and drink,
for there is the sound of abundance of rain.
AMP

October 11

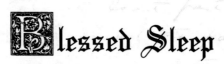

Blessed Sleep

Psalm 3:5

*I laid me down and slept; I awaked; for
the Lord sustained me.*

KJV

The Open Rock

Deuteronomy 2:7
For the Lord thy God hath blessed
thee in all the works of thy hand: he knows the wilderness
you have walked through and that you have lacked nothing.
Author's Paraphrase

October 13

Washing Away Bad

Ecclesiastes 7:8
Better is the end of a thing than the beginning thereof:
and the patient in spirit is better than the proud in spirit.
KJV

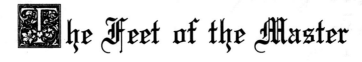

The Feet of the Master

Luke 10:39
And she had a sister called Mary, which also
sat at Jesus' feet, and heard his word.
KJV

October 15

 tanding on Holy Ground

Exodus 3:5
And he said, Draw not nigh hither: put off thy shoes from off thy
feet, for the place whereon thou standest is holy ground.
KJV

October 16

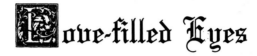

Love-filled Eyes

Isaiah 60:3
Nations will come to your light, and kings
to the brightness of your dawn.
NIV

October 17

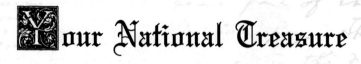

Your National Treasure

Jeremiah 30:8
'In that day,' declares the Lord Almighty, 'I will break the yoke off
their necks and will tear off their bonds...'
NIV

The Yoke of Light

Matthew 11:29-30
Take my yoke upon you and learn from me,
for I am gentle and humble in heart, and you will find rest for
your souls. For my yoke is easy and my burden is light.
NIV

October 19

Recalibrated

Romans 6:4
We were buried therefore with him by baptism into death, in order that, just as Christ was raised from the dead by the glory of the Father, we too might walk in newness of life.
ESV

The Door of Faith

Acts 14:27
And when they arrived and gathered the church
together, they declared all that God had done with them, and
how he had opened a door of faith to the Gentiles.
ESV

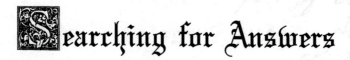

earching for Answers

Proverbs 2:3-5

Yea, if thou criest after knowledge, and liftest up thy voice for un-
derstanding; If thou seekest her as silver, and searchest
for her as for hid treasures; Then shalt thou understand
the fear of the Lord, and find the knowledge of God.
KJV

The High Life

2 Chronicles 32:30
And Hezekiah prospered in all his works for God
gave him great honor and wealth for he sought the Lord.
Author's Paraphrase

October 23

The Drawn Sword

Deuteronomy 20:3-4
...let not your hearts faint, fear not,
and do not tremble, neither be ye terrified because of them;
For the Lord your God is he that goeth with you, to fight
for you against your enemies, to save you.
KJV

October 24

 Heart of Forgiveness

Matthew 6:14
For if ye forgive men their trespasses,
your heavenly Father will also forgive you.
KJV

October 25

The Battle Gear of Victory

Isaiah 9:2
The people walking in darkness have seen a great light; on those
living in the land of the shadow of death a light has dawned.
NIV

October 26

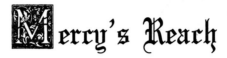

Mercy's Reach

Galatians 6:7
Be not deceived; God is not mocked: for
whatsoever a man soweth, that shall he also reap.
KJV

October 27

oven

Psalm 139:15

My substance was not hid from thee, when I was made in secret, and curiously wrought in the lowest parts of the earth.
KJV

The Lying Mirrors

Jonah 2:8
They that observe lying vanities forsake their own mercy.
KJV

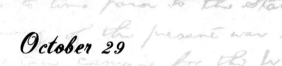

October 29

Destiny's Home

Isaiah 42:9
Behold, the former things are come to pass, and new
things do I declare: before they spring forth I tell you of them.
KJV

October 30

Dreaming

Numbers 12:6
And he said, Hear now my words: If there be
a prophet among you, I the Lord will make myself known unto
him in a vision, and will speak unto him in a dream.
KJV

October 31

Old Wineskins

Matthew 9:17
Neither do men put new wine into old bottles: else
the bottles break, and the wine runneth out, and the bottles perish:
but they put new wine into new bottles, and both are preserved.
KJV

From Useless Ashes

Isaiah 61:3
To appoint unto them that mourn in Zion, to give unto
them beauty for ashes, the oil of joy for mourning, the garment of
praise for the spirit of heaviness; that they might be called trees of
righteousness, the planting of the Lord, that he might be glorified.
KJV

November 2

Burning Coals

Leviticus 16:12
*And he shall take a censer full of burning coals
of fire from off the altar before the Lord, and his hands full of
sweet incense beaten small, and bring it within the vail.*
KJV

Unknown Power

Psalm 68:35
O God, thou art terrible out of thy holy places:
the God of Israel is he that giveth strength and power
unto his people. Blessed be God.
KJV

November 4

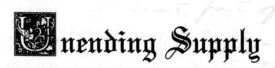

Unending Supply

Nehemiah 9:21
Yea, forty years didst thou sustain them
in the wilderness, so that they lacked nothing; their clothes
waxed not old, and their feet swelled not.
KJV

What You Value

1 Samuel 30:8
And David enquired at the Lord, saying, Shall I pursue after this
troop? shall I overtake them? And he answered him, Pursue: for thou
shalt surely overtake them, and without fail recover all.
KJV

November 6

When Faith Is Kneeling

Hebrews 11:6
But without faith it is impossible to please him:
for he that cometh to God must believe that he is, and that
he is a rewarder of them that diligently seek him.
KJV

November 7

Castaways

Genesis 14:16
And he brought back all the goods, and also
brought again his brother Lot, and his goods, and the
women also, and the people.
KJV

The Watered Soul

Psalm 84:6
Passing through the valley of weeping,
they make it a place of showers; the early
rain also fills the pools with blessings.
Author's Paraphrase

November 9

 # Kneeling Heart

Deuteronomy 4:29
But if from thence thou shalt seek the
Lord thy God, thou shalt find him, if thou seek him
with all thy heart and with all thy soul.
KJV

November 10

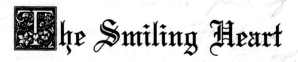

The Smiling Heart

Psalm 30:11
Thou hast turned for me my mourning into dancing:
thou hast put off my sackcloth, and girded me with gladness.
KJV

November 11

 I Am Watching

Deuteronomy 32:10
I will scan you and watch over
you as the apple of My eye.
Author's Paraphrase

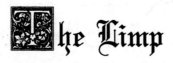he Limp

Zephaniah 3:19
I will deal with all who afflict you;
I will heal the limping ones.
Author's Paraphrase

Filling Infinity

James 1:17
*Every good gift and every perfect gift is from
above, and cometh down from the Father of lights, with whom
is no variableness, neither shadow of turning.*
KJV

#

Proverbs 28:27
He that giveth unto the poor shall not lack:
but he that hideth his eyes shall have many a curse.
KJV

The Finished Jar

1 Thessalonians 5:24
Faithful is he that calleth you,
who will also bring it to pass.
Author's Paraphrase

November 16

Diligence

Proverbs 22:29
Do you see a man diligent in his
work, he shall stand before kings...
Author's Paraphrase

holeness

Galatians 3:13
*Christ hath redeemed us from the curse of the law,
being made a curse for us: for it is written, Cursed
is every one that hangeth on a tree.*
KJV

In Solitude Defined

James 4:8
Draw nigh to God, and he will draw nigh to you...
KJV

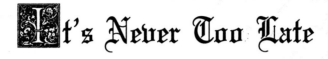t's Never Too Late

Isaiah 40:29
He gives power to the faint and weary,
and to him who has no might He increases strength
[causing it to multiply and making it to abound].
AMP

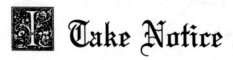

Take Notice

Galatians 6:9-10
And let us not be weary in well doing: for in
due season we shall reap, if we faint not. As we have therefore
opportunity, let us do good unto all men, especially unto
them who are of the household of faith.
KJV

November 21

Slaying the Prophets of Baal

1 Kings 18:40
Take the prophets of Baal, let no
one escape. And they took them, and Elijah slew them there.
Author's Paraphrase

Joy Addict

Psalm 51:12
*Restore to me the joy of my salvation
and uphold me with a free spirit.*
Author's Paraphrase

November 23

The Lights Are On

Psalm 18:28
For thou wilt light my candle: the Lord my
God will enlighten my darkness.
KJV

November 24

Longings of Heaven

Psalm 37:4
Delight yourself also in the Lord, And He
shall give you the desires of your heart.
NKJV

November 25

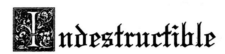

Indestructible

Matthew 7:25
And the rain descended, and the flood
came, and the winds blew, and beat upon that house;
and it fell not: for it was founded upon a rock.
KJV

The Billboard of Heaven

2 Kings 6:17
The Lord opened his eyes and he saw the mountain
was full of chariots of horses or fire round about Elisha.
Author's Paraphrase

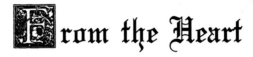

From the Heart

Proverbs 4:23
Keep and guard your heart with all vigilance and
above all that you guard, for out of it flow the springs of life.
AMP

November 28

Wear Your Armor

Ephesians 6:11
Put on the whole armor of God, that you may
be able to stand against the wiles of the devil.
NKJV

November 29

The Unflinching Soul

2 Thessalonians 2:2
Do not allow your minds to be quickly
unsettled or disturbed, whether it be by some [pretended]
revelation of [the] Spirit or by word or by letter.
Author's Paraphrase

The Fibers of Your Heart

Romans 4:19
He did not weaken in faith when he considered the
[utter] impotence of his own body, which was as good as dead
because he was about a hundred years old, or [when he considered]
the barrenness of Sarah's [deadened] womb.
AMP

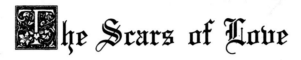

December 1

The Scars of Love

Isaiah 53:5
But he was wounded for our transgressions, he
was bruised for our iniquities: the chastisement of our peace
was upon him; and with his stripes we are healed.
KJV

 Divine Reversals

Isaiah 43:2
When thou passest through the waters, I will be
with thee; and through the rivers, they shall not overflow
thee: when thou walkest through the fire, thou shalt not
be burned; neither shall the flame kindle upon thee.
KJV

The Music of Your Soul

Psalm 91:4-5
He shall cover thee with his feathers, and under his wings shalt thou
trust: his truth shall be thy shield and buckler. Thou shalt not be
afraid for the terror by night; nor for the arrow that flieth by day.
KJV

December 4

Your Very Breath

Psalm 105:24
And he increased his people greatly; and
made them stronger than their enemies.
KJV

_____
_____
_____
_____
_____
_____
_____
_____
_____
_____
_____
_____
_____
_____
_____
_____
_____
_____
_____
_____

December 5

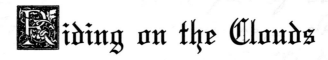

Riding on the Clouds

Isaiah 62:1
For Zion's sake will I not hold my peace, and for Jerusalem's sake I will not rest, until the righteousness thereof go forth as brightness, and the salvation thereof as a lamp that burneth.
KJV

December 6

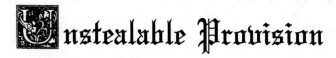

Unstealable Provision

1 Samuel 30:24
For who will hearken unto you in this matter?
but as his part is that goeth down to the battle, so shall his part
be that tarrieth by the stuff: they shall part alike.
KJV

In the Shadow of Peace

Matthew 6:25
Therefore I tell you, do not be anxious
about your life, what you will eat or what you will drink,
nor about your body, what you will put on. Is not life more
than food, and the body more than clothing?
ESV

The Pen of Good News

Psalm 112:7
He will not be afraid of evil tidings;
His heart is steadfast, trusting in the Lord.
NKJV

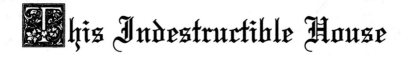his Indestructible House

Deuteronomy 33:28
So Israel lived in safety, in a land of
grain and wine, whose heavens drop down dew.
ESV

December 10

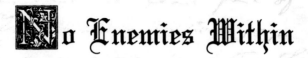

No Enemies Within

John 14:30
*I will not talk with you much more, for the prince
of the world is coming. And he has no claim on Me. [He has
nothing in common with Me; there is nothing in Me that
belongs to him, and he has no power over Me.]*
AMP

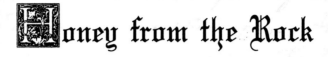Honey from the Rock

Deuteronomy 32:13
I will make you drink honey
from the rock, and oil out of the flinty rock.
Author's Paraphrase

Bring Your Vessels

2 Kings 4:3
Then he said, "Go, borrow vessels
from everywhere, from all your neighbors -
empty vessels; do not gather just a few.
NKJV

December 13

The Center

Philippians 3:7
But what things were gain to me,
those I counted loss for Christ.
KJV

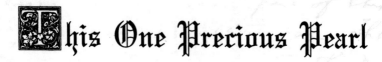his One Precious Pearl

Matthew 13:45-46
Again the kingdom of heaven is like a man
who on finding a precious pearl, sold
everything he had and bought it.
Author's Paraphrase

The Sound of Your Sickle

Revelation 14:18
Put forth your sickle and reap the
ripe fruit I have prepared for you.
Author's Paraphrase

December 16

Wild Grapes

Micah 4:4
*But they shall sit every man under his vine and
under his fig tree; and none shall make them afraid...*
KJV

December 17

The Devil's Teeth

Psalm 46:9
He makes wars cease to the end of
the earth; He breaks the bow and cuts the spear
in two; He burns the chariots in the fire.
NKJV

December 18

Keep On Rowing

Psalm 66:12
...we went through fire and through water, but
You brought us out into a broad, moist place [to
abundance and refreshment and the open air].
AMP

December 19

Chase Me

Song of Solomon 1:2
We will run after you, for
your Love is better than wine.
Author's Paraphrase

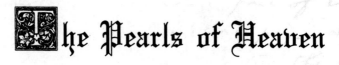

The Pearls of Heaven

Proverbs 28:27
He who gives to the poor will not lack, but
he who hides his eyes will have many curses.
NKJV

The Champion Inside You

Philippians 4:13
I can do all things through Christ
who strengthens me.
NKJV

December 22

Abba Father

Romans 8:15
For ye have not received the spirit of
bondage again to fear; but ye have received the
Spirit of adoption, whereby we cry, Abba, Father.
KJV

Just In Time

Psalm 116:7-8
Return unto thy rest, O my soul;
for the Lord hath dealt bountifully with thee.
For thou hast delivered my soul from death, mine
eyes from tears, and my feet from falling.
KJV

December 24

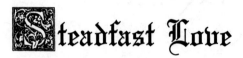

Steadfast Love

Lamentations 3:22-23
The steadfast love of the Lord never
ceases, his mercies never come to an end; they are
new every morning; great is thy faithfulness.
RSV

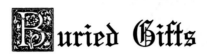

Buried Gifts

Proverbs 18:16
A man's gift maketh room for him,
and bringeth him before great men.
KJV

December 26

And the Dove Came Back

Genesis 8:11
And the dove came back to him
in the evening, and behold, in her mouth
was a freshly plucked olive leaf...
ESV

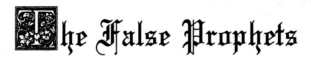The False Prophets

1 Kings 18:40
And Elijah said unto them, Take the
prophets of Baal; let not one of them escape.
And they took them: and Elijah brought them
down to the brook Kishon, and slew them there.
KJV

December 28

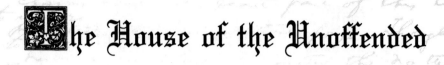

The House of the Unoffended

Psalm 119:165
Great peace have they which love thy law:
and nothing shall offend them.
KJV

December 29

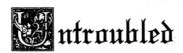

Untroubled

Philippians 4:9
Practice what you have learned and received and heard and seen in Me, and model your way of living on it, and the God of peace (of untroubled, undisturbed well-being) will be with you.
AMP

The Nectar of Life

1 Peter 1:8
Without having seen Him, we love Him,
without having seen him we believe in Him and we exalt
and are thrilled with inexpressible and glorious joy.
Author's Paraphrase

Live Your Life
with Open Hands

Genesis 39:3
And his master saw that the Lord was
with him and that the Lord made all that
he did to flourish and succeed in his hand.
AMP

Experience
What Matters

download the Ivan Tait App

be mentored by Ivan
enroll in virtual university
purchase more products
sign-up for Ivan's emails
stay informed

meet our children

meet our widows
help turn orphans into
R O Y A L T Y
go to Guatemala

CPSIA information can be obtained at www.ICGtesting.com
Printed in the USA
LVOW10s0909191214

PP9164400001B/7/P